What's in this book

This book belongs to

_____

我们都一样 We are the Same

学习内容 Contents

沟通 Communication

说说五官

Talk about parts of the face

生词 New words

★ 头	head
★ 耳朵	ear
★ 眼睛	eye
★ 鼻子	nose
★ 嘴巴	mouth
这	this
是	to be
的	of

句式 Sentence patterns

这是我的头。
This is my head.

这是他的嘴巴。
This is his mouth.

这是她的鼻子。
This is her nose.

跨学科学习 Project

认识视觉、听觉、嗅觉、味觉及相应的器官
Learn about the senses and the corresponding parts of the face

文化 Cultures

中国的眼保健操
Chinese eye exercises

Get ready

1 How many of your friends have black hair?

2 How are we different? How are we the same?

3 Which part of the face do you like most?

tóu
头

这是我的头。

ěr duo

耳朵

这是我的耳朵。

这是他的眼睛。

鼻子
bí zi

这是她的鼻子。

嘴巴

这是我们的嘴巴。

我们不一样，我们都一样。

Let's think

1 Look carefully. Circle the parts of the child's face.

2 Look at the pictures and listen to your teacher. Put a tick or a cross.

1 这是她的嘴巴。 ☐

2 这是他的耳朵。 ☐

3 这是她的鼻子。 ☐

New words

1 Learn the new words.

头

眼睛

鼻子

耳朵

嘴巴

这是我的。

2 Draw arrows to label the clown's face. Colour the balloons.

头

眼睛

鼻子

耳朵

嘴巴

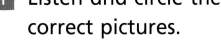
听听说说 Listen and say

🎧 **03** **1** Listen and circle the correct pictures.

1

2

3

4
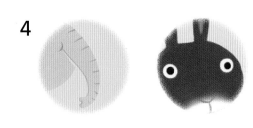

🎧 **04** **2** Look at the pictures. Listen to the sto

① 这是我和姐姐。我们的鼻子一样。

③ 我们的眼睛、鼻子和耳朵都一样。

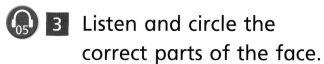

3 Listen and circle the correct parts of the face.

1

2

3

4

4 Talk with your friend.

Task

Paste your photo and talk about it.

这是我的小狗。

这是我的爸爸和妈妈。
这是我的弟弟。

这是我的姐姐。她叫
依依。她十岁。

Paste your photo here.

Game

Listen to your teacher and draw the monsters' faces.

Song

 06 Listen and sing.

头、眼睛、耳朵、鼻子、嘴巴。

头、眼睛、耳朵、鼻子、嘴巴。

我们有眼睛、耳朵、鼻子、嘴巴，

我们都一样呀，都一样。

课堂用语 Classroom language

再说一遍。	再读一遍。	再来一次。	跟我读。
Say it again.	Read it again.	And again.	Read after me.

写一写 Write

1 Learn and trace the stroke.

横折

2 Learn the component. Circle 目 in the appropriate characters.

目　朗　眼　晴　睛

3 Circle and count 目 . Write the number at the centre of the target board.

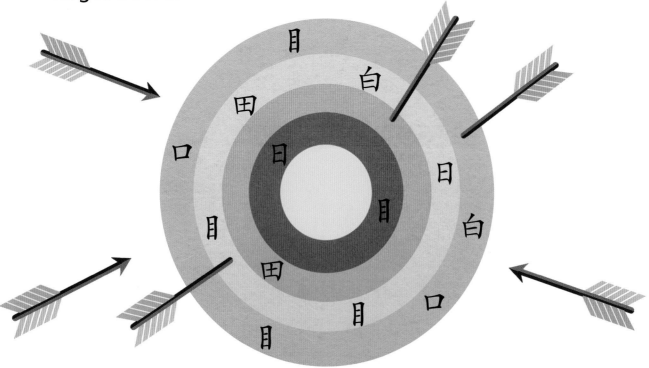

4 Trace and write the character.

眼

眼	眼	眼

5 Write and say.

这是小狗的 ⬚ 睛。

汉字小常识 Did you know?

Many components give clues to the meaning of the character.

Learn about how the characters are related to 目.

目				眠
eye	blind	see	eyebrow	sleep

Cultures

Take good care of your eyes. Learn about the Chinese eye exercises.

Eye exercises are widely practised in schools in China as a method to help students take good care of their eyes and prevent short-sightedness.

Follow the steps. Massage your eyes with your fingers.

①

Under your eyebrows

②

Near your nose

③

On your cheeks

④

Around your eyes

1 Complete the sentences. Write the letters.

看
see

听
hear

a 鼻子

b 嘴巴

c 眼睛

d 耳朵

我用＿＿＿看。

我用＿＿＿听。

闻
smell

尝
taste

我用＿＿＿闻。

我用＿＿＿尝。

2 Make funny faces with fruit and vegetables.

这是她的嘴巴。

这是他的眼睛。

这是他的耳朵。

 温习 Checkpoint

1 Answer the questions from children around the world.

我七岁。你几岁？

你叫什么名字？

What are these?

Can you say 'hello' in Chinese?

你好！

Can you write 'eye' in Chinese?

This is my mouth.

How do you say this in Chinese?

Can you point to my 鼻子?

Can you read this sentence aloud?

这是我的爸爸和妈妈。

Can you point to my 耳朵?

2 Work with your friend. Colour the stars and the chillies.

Words and sentences	说	读	写
头	☆	☆	🌶
耳朵	☆	☆	🌶
眼睛	☆	☆	🌶
鼻子	☆	☆	🌶
嘴巴	☆	☆	🌶
这	☆	🌶	🌶
是	☆	🌶	🌶
的	☆	🌶	🌶
这是我的头。	☆	☆	🌶

Talk about parts of the face	☆

3 What does your teacher say?

My teacher says …

分享 Sharing

Words I remember

头		tóu	head
耳	朵	ěr duo	ear
眼	睛	yǎn jing	eye
鼻	子	bí zi	nose
嘴	巴	zuǐ ba	mouth
这		zhè	this
是		shì	to be
的		de	of

Other words

我们	wǒ men	we, us
都	dōu	both, all
不	bù	not
一样	yī yàng	same

Oxford University Press is a department of the University of Oxford.
It furthers the University's objective of excellence in research, scholarship,
and education by publishing worldwide. Oxford is a registered trade mark of
Oxford University Press in the UK and in certain other countries

Published in Hong Kong by
Oxford University Press (China) Limited
39th Floor, One Kowloon, 1 Wang Yuen Street, Kowloon Bay,
Hong Kong

First Edition published in 2017

Illustrated by Anne Lee and Wildman

Photographs for reproduction permitted by Dreamstime.com

China National Publications Import & Export (Group) Corporation is an authorized distributor of
Oxford Elementary Chinese.

Please contact content@cnpiec.com.cn or 86-10-65856782

ISBN: 978-0-19-082140-1

10 9 8 7 6 5 4 3 2